LOVING GOD'S WORD AS JESUS DID

by Randy Southern

Published by Cook Ministry Resources
a division of Cook Communications Ministries

4050 Lee Vance View
Colorado Springs, Colorado 80918

Colorado Springs, CO/Paris, Ontario
www.cookministries.com
Printed in U.S.A.

Author: Randy Southern
Designer: Rebekah Lyon
Editorial Team: Cheryl Crews, Matthew Eckmann, Janna Jones, Gary Wilde, Gayle Wise, Vicki Witte

TABLE OF CONTENTS

WHY DISCIPLESHIP?

Discipleship is a well-worn word. It's been used to justify everything from programs to events. But have you ever wondered what was in the mind of God when He invented the whole concept? His infinite wisdom could have created any method to accomplish His purpose in our lives. But this all-wise God simply told us to "make disciples."

Though there are many definitions for it, we could all agree that discipleship includes the process of learning and following Christ. And the bottom line is to become like Jesus, right? As Christians, we talk a lot about doing and not enough about being (God made us human beings, not human "doings"). He desires us to be conformed to the image of His Son (Romans 8:29). That process begins at salvation and continues until we arrive on heaven's shore.

So why disciple teenagers? Why not another program or "instant growth" gimmick? Why not entertainment or the newest ministry fad? Why discipleship?

First, because students need it. Pick up your newspaper or take a walk through the halls of your local high school if you need motivation. Second, Jesus commanded and modeled it. And third, history confirms it. Put simply, it works. It avoids the prevalent quick-fix, "decision" mentality and focuses instead on a long-term lifestyle. Discipleship is not a program. It's God's plan. It involves sharing with your students both the Word and your life, which leaves a lasting impact (1 Thessalonians 2:7-8).

Discipling teenagers doesn't require that they be good-looking, intelligent, well-balanced or popular (think of the original dozen in Jesus' group!). It only requires students who are faithful learners and willing followers of Christ.

Some might say teenagers aren't ready for discipleship, that they can't handle the meat of the Word or the challenge of following Christ. Theirs is sort of a "junior Christianity." They don't have what it takes to become great for God. But we know better, don't we? Sid do Joseph, David, Daniel, Shadrach, Meshach, Abednego, Mary, and John Mark.

So does God.

The original Twelve disciples weren't much when they began, but they changed the course of human history. If we only had the first part of their story, we wouldn't hold out much hope for them—knowing their frequent faults and failures. But you know the rest of the story. The same is true for your students. The rest of their story is yet to be written. That's where you come in. This book is actually divided into two parts: Part One is contained in the following pages. But Part Two is yet to be written—and God has given you the opportunity to be part of writing that story as you touch your students' hearts with your life day by day.

This world desperately needs Christian youth to rise up and to answer the call of Christ to "come follow Me." This book will help them do that.

So pour your life into them. Impart the Word to them. Believe in them. Don't give up on them. Disciple them. And most of all,

Enjoy the journey!
Jeff Kinley

WHY CUSTOM DISCIPLESHIP?

So, you're convinced that what your students need is discipleship. So, why *Custom Discipleship?* Because *Custom Discipleship* acknowledges and deals with the two seemingly contradictory but central truths of discipleship.

1. There are Biblical principles that remain constant for all disciples of Jesus.
Custom Discipleship teaches students about the life of Christ and the example He set for Christians. Those stories are unchanging. The truths that Jesus communicated through word and example are the principles by which all Christians can truly live.

2. Discipleship is a dynamic, ever-changing process.
Custom Discipleship provides options that allow you to customize the learning process to meet the needs of the students in your group—no matter where they are in their relationship with Christ. This ability to customize the material keeps it dynamic and relevant to the lives of your students. Each lesson also contains *Learner Links* and *Making it Real* discipleship tips to help small-group leaders learn to share their lives with students and to grow alongside the students they are leading.

Custom Discipleship is a curriculum designed to blend the power of these truths. Let it help you as you take the challenge of discipling youth and obey Christ's command to make disciples.

Jeff Kinley is a veteran student minister, dedicated to students, parents, and youthworkers as a life calling. He is the author of several successful books, including No Turning Back, Never the Same *and* Done Deal, *(David C. Cook Church Resources). A gifted communicator, Jeff is a frequent speaker at conferences and youth camps. Jeff and his wife Beverly, have three sons—Clayton, Stuart and Davis.*

KEY QUESTIONS

are the focus of the lesson. Students should be able to answer these by the end of the session.

BIBLE BASE gives the

scripture references that are the basis for the whole session.

THE OPENER is

optional to the session. It is a great way to get kids involved before diving into the study.

SESSION **3**

WHAT A SERVANT FEELS

Key Questions
• How do our own painful experiences equip us to help others who are hurting?
• What kind of an example did Jesus set when it came to empathizing with people who are hurting?
• How can you empathize with hurting people?

Bible Base
Matthew 25:31-46
John 11:1-44
Romans 12:15

Supplies
• Flip chart
• Pens
• Pencils or pens
• Index cards
• Copies of Resources 3A, 3B, and Journal

Opener (Optional)

Common Ground
Ask your students to pull their chairs into a circle. Choose one of your group members to start the game standing in the middle of the circle. Remove his or her chair from the circle (think Musical Chairs). The person in the middle will call out a category. The category may be anything from "Collects comic books" to "Born in another state" to "Hates country music." Everyone in the group who fits the category must stand up and run to an empty seat. The person in the middle, meanwhile, must also try to get to an open chair. The person who doesn't make it must then stand in the middle of the circle and call out the next category.

LEARNER LINK
This Link activity is designed to stretch your students' brains a bit. Many of the answers on Resource 3A may sound very close to correct but are not the best answers. Watch to see how deeply your students struggle with the issue of suffering. This question has been asked through the centuries, and there is no easy answer.

MAKING IT REAL
As you get to know your students better, pray for them specifically. Taking the time to do this will help you to focus on their needs. It will also help you to continually acknowledge and trust that it is God who is making these kids into disciples of Jesus Christ—sometimes even in spite of your efforts!

This activity may prove to be an effective bonding exercise for your group members. They may be surprised to find out that other people in the group share their interests, experiences, or background.

CUSTOM DISCIPLESHIP 33

SUPPLIES listed here

are those needed for the core lesson. Any supplies for options are listed with that optional activity.

BOLD TYPE signifies "teacher

talk"—things to be said directly by the leader of the group.

THERE ARE THREE LINKS that

divide each session, taking students through the learning process and into personal application.

LEARNER LINKS

are located through the sessions to give the leader extra tips on how to help their students learn the Word of God.

MAKING IT REAL

sections are tips on discipleship located throughout the sessions.

After your group members have weighed in on the topic of Jesus' empathy, ask: Maybe one of the reasons God allows us to experience pain, suffering, loss, and hard times is so that we will be better able to understand what other hurting people are going through and be better prepared to help them? Why or why not? Let your group members offer their opinions.

Link 3

Empathy 'n' Me
Ask: Have you ever had someone say to you, "I know just how you're feeling"? If so, how did you feel when you heard those words? Did you believe the person? Why or why not? These words are especially popular at funerals. Usually the people who use the phrase don't mean any disrespect by it; they just might not know what else to say.

What if the person really did know how you feel—somewhat, at least? What if he or she had gone through a similar experience? Would you be interested in talking to that person? Why?

After a few students have offered their thoughts, say: Okay, let's reverse the situation. Let's say you run into someone who's hurting or in need of help. Let's say that the person is going through a situation similar to one you went through a year or so ago. Would you be interested in talking to that person? If some of your group members express reluctance, listen to their reasons for not getting involved. Invite the rest of the group to respond to those reasons.

The resource sheet "What I've Got to Give" (Resource 3B) is designed to help your group members identify the things in their lives that qualify them to be truly empathetic, the situations and circumstances they've experienced that make them experts of sorts in dealing with specific kinds of hurt. Encourage your students to take this assignment seriously. Emphasize that no one will be asked to share anything on the sheet that he or she is uncomfortable with.

LEARNER LINK
If any of your group members are brave enough to share their responses to Resource 3B, you will need to respect their feelings, as well as their privacy. You may need to ask a few questions to clarify a point or to correct a possible misunderstanding, but try not to pry for more information. Do not put your students in a position where they feel pressure to reveal more than they want to. When your volunteers finish sharing, be quick to affirm them, and encourage the rest of the group to do the same.

MAKING IT REAL
A big part of discipleship is encouraging your students to put what they have learned into action. As their leader, you should be constantly looking for teachable moments—times when you are together with the students, outside of your group time, in which you can encourage them to practice what they have been learning. Another great way to do this is to set up service projects or experiential learning times. Session five in this book provides what you need to set up one of these learning experiences.

After a few minutes, ask if there are any volunteers who would like to share some of the things they wrote down. After the volunteers have shared, discuss as a group the possibility that there are people in this world who can benefit from the negative things that have happened to us.

Before you wrap up this session, throw out a few more questions to the group: What if you run into someone who's facing a problem you've never encountered? Let's say you've never had any experience with this kind of problem. Can you still offer that person empathy? If so, how?

36 CUSTOM DISCIPLESHIP

OPTION ICONS are

located at the beginning of each link to let you know that there are options for those groups at the end of the session.

RESOURCE PAGES are

noted throughout the session. The actual pages are reproducible and can be found at the end of each session.

JOURNAL

HEART CHECK:
A Practical Approach to Recognizing Hurt
You may think you've picked up some valuable tips for becoming aware of hurting people, but unless you actually put those tips to use in your life, they're useless. Keep in mind that Jesus was not only "listeners" of His Word, but "doers" (James 1:22). This sheet is for doers.

LOOK IT UP! is a section of the student journal page that encourages kids to continue their process of discipleship through the week. It provides a passage of Scripture and a question for each day of the week.

LOOK IT UP
Below you'll find seven Scripture references, one for every day of the week. Each passage listed below has something interesting to say about people who are hurting or in need. Spend a few minutes each day looking up the passage and writing down a few (relevant) ideas that pop into your head.

▶ **DAY ONE:** Mark 2:13-17 (What example did Jesus set when it comes to recognizing people in need?)

▶ **DAY TWO:** Ephesians 5:1-2 (How would an imitator of God respond to hurting people?)

☺ TALK IT UP
Jesus assures us that "all things are possible with God" (Mark 10:27). That includes spotting the needs of other people. So when you're looking for other people's needs, a wise first step is to talk to God about it. Take some time to write down a few prayer requests, specific ways in which you need the Lord to help you focus more intently on those who are hurting. (For example, you might ask Him to help you shift your focus away from yourself.) Don't be afraid to get personal here. No one else needs to see your request list.

TALK IT UP! provides a place to write down personal prayer requests as well as the needs of accountability partners.

DO IT UP! provides a chance for personal application. It contains a *Plan!* and *Act!* and a *Review!* section to help students put what they learn into practice.

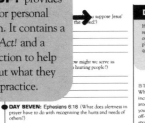

DO IT UP
If you're serious about learning to recognize the needs and hurts of other people, you'll need an action plan. Just answer the following questions.

STEP **ONE: Plan!**
What steps will you take this week to increase your awareness of the people around you? Put some thought into your response. Don't just give vague, off-the-top-of-your-head answers. Be specific. What exactly are you planning to do? When will you do it?

▶ **DAY SEVEN:** Ephesians 6:18 (What does alertness in prayer have to do with recognizing the hurts and needs of others?)

CHECKLIST of options allows you to keep track of which options you have used.

Planning Checklist
LINK 1: What Do You See?
❑ Advanced Learners
❑ Media
❑ Extra Adrenaline
❑ Junior High

LINK 2: The Needs Around Jesus
❑ Little Bible Background
❑ Advanced Learners
❑ Mostly Guys
❑ Mostly Girls

LINK 3: See the Hurt
❑ Little Bible Background
❑ Mostly Guys
❑ Mostly Girls
❑ Media
❑ Extra Adrenaline
❑ Junior High

20 CUSTOM DISCIPLESHIP

OPTIONS are designed for specific types of groups but provide great variety if you want to mix and match.

SESSION **1** OPTIONS

LITTLE BIBLE BACKGROUND
Link 2
If your students have trouble picturing the Son of God, Jesus, as a flesh-and-blood person, review a few Scripture passages that illustrate His humanity. He was conceived supernaturally apart from any human father, but He was born naturally of a human mother (Matt. 1:18). He grew like a normal child, both physically and mentally (Luke 2:40). He experienced hunger (Matt. 4:2) and thirst (John 19:28). He got tired after long journeys (John 4:6). He required sleep (Matt. 8:24).

Link 3
If your group members aren't familiar at all with God's Word, you may want to spend a minute or two reviewing the second-most important command in all of Scripture. Read Matthew 22:39. Ask: Do you think it's possible to love other people as much as you love yourself? If so, how would you show that love in your day-to-day actions? Suggest that this kind of love requires a change of priorities, from a self-centered perspective to an others-centered perspective.

ADVANCED LEARNERS
Link 1
Here's a tough challenge for your Bible know-it-alls: Name three people in the Bible who were oblivious—either by choice or by circumstances—to the needs and hurts of people around them. Students might suggest people like the priest and the Levite in the story of the good Samaritan, who left an injured man lying in the road while they went about their business.

Link 2
If your students are used to responding to questions that have obvious or "right" answers, cross...

EACH ICON represents a type of group and designates options specific for that group.

THIS HEADING tells the section of the session where this option can be used.

①

LEARN IT WELL!

KEY QUESTIONS

- What is the role of the Bible in the Christian life?
- How did Jesus affirm the need for learning God's Word?
- How can you benefit from the wisdom and experience of others when it comes to understanding God's Word?

BIBLE BASE

Luke 2:41-52

SUPPLIES

- Paper
- Pencils
- Bibles
- Copies of Resources 1A, 1B, Journal

Opener (Optional)

What's Biblical about Christianity?

Start your meeting by forming two teams. Let everyone know that the first team is to come up with statements that describe "the Christian life." The other team is to "censor" the statements if they do not refer to anything that is taught in the Bible. In other words, the trick for team one is to name aspects of Christian living that are *not* found in the Bible at all. Award points to the teams for statements that were either censored or not.

LEARNER LINK

Recruit a couple of your group members for an activity called "Student Teachers." Each of your recruits will give a brief how-to demonstration of a skill he or she knows. One person may show the group how to change a tire (using an actual jack and tire, for visual effect). Another person may demonstrate CPR or the Heimlech Maneuver. Still another may show the group how to juggle. Interview each teacher to find out how he or she learned these skills.

Afterward, hold a brief discussion with the group, using the following questions:
- **Was it hard or easy to come up with descriptions of Christian living unrelated to the Bible's teachings?**
- **How important would you say the Bible is to the Christian faith?**
- **How important is God's Word to youth? Why?**

Make the transition to Link 1 by saying: **Let's look a little closer at what we learn in life and how we learn it.**

MAKING IT REAL

For the next four or five weeks, you will be teaching your students what it means to be disciples of Jesus Christ. One of the most helpful things you can do to help them grow as disciples is to assign "accountability partners." Explain to your group members that, for the next few weeks, accountability partners will be responsible for checking on and encouraging each other's growth as disciples. The partners should plan on hooking up at least twice a week (whether at school or by phone) to update each other on their discipleship efforts.

Link 1

AVID LEARNERS

Hand out copies of "What's the Source of Your Smarts?" (Resource 1A). Give group members a few minutes to complete the sheet. When they're finished, ask volunteers to share their responses. Encourage your students to talk about their early education and discuss common experiences. Then start a discussion with them about learning.

How do we learn? Some answers include listening, asking questions, critical thinking, paying attention, taking risks.

What have you learned in the last three days? (This should be an easy one for the students, since we all learn new things everyday, from new ways to drive around your city or town, to new information learned in school.) **What if someone said that he or she hasn't learned anything in the last three days? Would you believe him or her? Why?**

What kind of character traits would someone need to be a good learner? A good learner would be concerned about learning and not showing off the knowledge he or she already has. A learner would need to understand what it means to persevere in order to learn, remember, and apply knowledge to his or her life. A learner would also be creative, courageous, and eager.

How do you recognize that you need to learn something?

Some things are harder for people to learn than others. Think of something that was hard for you to learn. Was it worth it? Why?

What would you say is the most important thing you've ever learned? How did you learn it? Why is it so important? Pause between each question to give your group a chance to think and respond.

If no one mentions it, ask: **Do we need God's Word in order to learn certain things? Is there any other way we could know about the Lord?** If you get some differing opinions here, make sure that people on each side of the issue get an opportunity to share their thoughts and feelings.

Link 2

JESUS LEARNED TOO!

Introduce the Bible study portion of your meeting with the following question:

Do you think Jesus had feelings similar to yours when He was learning something? Why or why not? Remind students that Jesus was born a baby and had to learn how to eat and dress Himself. We really don't know how Jesus felt during this time in His life because the Bible doesn't mention these details, but this question will help students see how Jesus can relate to them even though He lived in a different century.

Did Jesus take time to learn about the Bible? This may seem like a trick question, but it's not. To supplement your students' answers, ask someone to read Luke 2:52 aloud. Discuss the different ways that Jesus grew, focusing on "wisdom."

Discuss: **What does it mean to grow in wisdom?** (It means to learn. This verse indicates that Jesus learned things while He was on earth. The fact that Jesus grew "in favor with God" suggests that He learned about God's Word. But beyond just learning, wisdom means the ability to apply God's Word to making good choices about life.)
Ask a couple of your group members to read Luke 2:41-51, trading off verses as they read. When they're finished, use the following questions and suggestions to guide your discussion of the passage:

Describe a normal 12-year-old. (Twelve can be an awkward age—not quite a child, not quite a teenager. It's also an age of curiosity, an age at which students intensify their observation and, therefore, their questioning of the world around them.) **What were you like when you were 12?** (Take responses and probe the students to get them to think about the ways they are different now compared to when they were 12.)

What was Jesus doing at the temple? (He was sitting among the teachers, listening and asking questions. In other words, He was involved in learning. He was learning from God, from God's Word, and from the people around Him.) **What would be the equivalent of that today?** (Going to a church and sitting in on the pastors' meeting. Spending some time in the "teacher's lounge" of a seminary or university, asking professors to explain more about God.)

Why were the people who heard the 12-year-old boy amazed? (The questions Jesus asked apparently showed that He had a much deeper understanding of God's Word than they expected. It's likely that Jesus was challenging the religious leaders in the temple as much as He was learning from them. Remember: Jesus is fully God and fully human. In choosing not to exercise His divine nature while on earth [at most times], He would have had to learn as other human beings learn. See Phil. 2:7)

What example did Jesus set for us when it comes to learning God's Word? (If Jesus could benefit from studying God's Word, then anyone can—and should. If we want to learn about God and His will for us, we need to read it for ourselves, regularly. We also need to put ourselves in a place where God's Word is being taught. We should challenge our teachers and interact with them, asking questions rather than sitting passively.)

What do you think would happen if we chose not to commit ourselves to learning God's Word? What if we were to rely on just our own limited knowledge? What do you think would happen to our spiritual lives? Encourage your students to think beyond a "formula" mentality. Often times, we choose to reduce learning God's Word to "devotions"—that once-a-day ritual that students endure because it fulfills their end of the bargain with God. Jesus knew that the Words of God were life, that gave Him—and still give us—the best way to live. God does not operate by formulas. He wants His Word living and active in us, not just series of verses read once a day designed to ensure His blessings.

IDEAL CANDIDATES

As we just studied, there are many things to learn and ways to learn. In fact each one of us has our own unique style of learning. One thing we need to remember is that it is important to direct our learning and submit our hearts to God in the process.

There are so many things we can learn about as we go through our lives. What are some good ways to learn about God's Word? (Going to church, listening to a pastor. Listening to praise music. Reading the Bible for yourself. Attending a Bible study or discipleship group like you are doing now.)

Notice that the ways to learn about God's Word involve a balance of personal study and interaction with other people. It is also important to think for yourself, have your own relationship with God, and have the characteristics of a learner. It is important to have relationships that can help your critical thinking and point you toward God.

Hand out copies of "Whadda Ya Lookin' For?" (Resource 1B). Tell your students that this sheet will help them think about the qualities they value in a teacher. Then give them a few minutes to complete the sheet. When they're finished, go through the list as a group.

Ask: **How did you rank each quality? Why? Which qualities are very important to you and which are not? What qualities were not included in this list?** Discuss which qualities are absolutely necessary and which ones are more a matter of personal preference.

LEARNER **LINK**

It will be helpful for each one of your students to have a discipleship notebook. You can create these using three-ring binders or simple file folders. (If your folders are the standard 8.5 x 11 you will need to copy the resource pages at 120%.) Encourage your students to keep all of the resource pages that they receive in this notebook. This will be especially helpful as they work through the daily readings and questions for the "Heart Check" pages. You may also want to provide some extra paper for them to use as journal pages. The whole purpose of this is to help your students see discipleship as an ongoing process and to help them continue to grow outside of the group.

MAKING IT R E A L

Encourage your students to share prayer requests with each other. You may want to have a specific time to do this as a group or encourage accountability partners to do it sometime during the week. Ask students to commit to praying for those requests. Encourage your students to include requests related to this session, including asking God to grow a deep love for His Word in each student.

Let's say you decide it might be helpful for you to find a mentor—or at least someone who can teach you a little more about God's Word or the Christian life. Based on the characteristics and qualities you selected on the sheet, who—or where—would you turn to? It's possible that your group members won't be able to come up with people who fit their criteria. If so, encourage them to broaden the scope of their thinking and turn to someone whom they normally wouldn't have much to do with. Suggest that they may be surprised at the people God uses to help them grow. Remind your students that consistent perseverance with God's Word comes from a variety of sources. While mentors may be hard to find, they can take advantage of a wise person who has written a book about aspects of the Christian life and how God uses them to teach people all over the world.

As you wrap up the session, hand out copies of the student journal, "Heart Check: A Practical Approach to Learning God's Word" (Resource 1C). The sheet is designed to motivate your group members to consider their need for a Christian mentor. Direct your students to the "Do It Up" section of the sheet and have them spend a few moments of class time answering the "Plan!" questions. Give them a few minutes of silent prayer and then have them share their next step with their accountability partner.

What's the Source of Your Smarts?

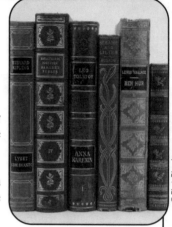

There are all kinds of things to learn in life. And we learn them from many sources. This little exercise will help you think about *how* you've learned the things you know.

Answer all of the questions below that apply to you. If there's something you haven't learned to do yet—like driving, for example—you can either leave the answer blank or write down who you think will teach you.

1. Who taught you how to eat?_____

2. How did you learn to ride a bike?_____

3. Where did you learn about "the birds and the bees"?_____

4. Who taught you how to drive?_____

5. How did you learn to speak a foreign language?_____

6. Where did you learn your first swear word?_____

7. How did you learn how to dress?_____

8. How did you learn what good music is?_____

9. Who taught you how to read?_____

10. How did you learn what to do with your money?_____

11. Who taught you about the importance of being honest?_____

12. How did you learn your table manners?_____

13. When did you learn that life isn't always fair?_____

14. How did you learn what Jesus is like?_____

15. Who taught you about the meaning of life?_____

Whadda Ya Lookin' For?

Below are ten qualities or characteristics that some people look for in a teacher. Rate each characteristic on a scale of one to five, based on how important it is to you that a potential teacher possess that quality. (One indicates that the quality is not very important at all; five indicates that the quality is extremely important.)

_____ 1. SOMEONE WHO IS FUNNY.

_____ 2. SOMEONE WHO HAS TEACHING EXPERIENCE.

_____ 3. SOMEONE WHO IS CLOSE TO MY OWN AGE.

_____ 4. SOMEONE WHO MAKES GOD'S WORD AND THE CHRISTIAN LIFE SEEM INTERESTING.

_____ 5. SOMEONE WHO HAS HIGH EXPECTATIONS FOR MY SPIRITUAL GROWTH.

_____ 6. SOMEONE WHO HAS STRUGGLED WITH HIS OR HER FAITH IN THE PAST.

_____ 7. SOMEONE WHO KNOWS ME WELL.

_____ 8. SOMEONE WHO IS RESPECTED IN THE CHURCH.

_____ 9. SOMEONE WHO IS CASUAL IN HIS OR HER APPROACH TO TEACHING.

_____ 10. SOMEONE WHO STAYS IN REGULAR CONTACT WITH ME THROUGHOUT THE WEEK.

© PhotoDisc, Inc.

HEART CHECK:
A Practical Approach to Learning God's Word

You may think you've picked up some valuable tips for learning God's Word, but unless you actually put those tips to use in your life, they're useless. Remember, God wants not only "listeners" of His Word, but "doers" (James 1:22). This sheet is for doers.

LOOK IT UP

Below you'll find seven Scripture references, one for every day of the week. Each passage listed below has something interesting to say about God's Word and teachers. Spend a few minutes each day looking up the passage and writing down a few (relevant) thoughts that pop into your head.

● **DAY ONE:** Hebrews 4:12 (God's Word is like what? What does that mean?)

_____
_____
_____
_____

● **DAY TWO:** Acts 11:25-26 (What kinds of things do you think Paul and Barnabas taught the early Christians?)

_____
_____
_____
_____

● **DAY THREE:** Proverbs 15:22 (Why are many advisers better than a few?)

_____
_____
_____
_____

● **DAY FOUR:** Titus 2:1-10 (What are some things you and other people your age need to learn?)

_____
_____
_____
_____

☻ TALK IT UP

Jesus assures us that "all things are possible with God" (Mark 10:27). That includes learning God's Word and finding people who will help you grow as a Christian. So when you're faced with doubts about allowing someone else to advise you, a wise first step is to talk to God about it. Take some time to write down a few prayer requests, specific ways in which you need the Lord to help you as you start. (For example, you might ask Him to help you find the right friends or teacher.) Don't be afraid to get personal here. No one else needs to see your request list.

_____
_____
_____
_____
_____
_____
_____
_____
_____
_____
_____
_____
_____
_____
_____
_____
_____

DAY FIVE: Psalm 119:105 (Are you surprised at how David described God's Word? Why or why not?)

_____

_____

_____

_____

DAY SIX: Acts 8:26-40 (What does this story tell us about God's feelings toward teaching and teachers?)

_____

_____

_____

_____

DAY SEVEN: Leviticus 10:8-11 (Do you think the Lord still chooses certain people today to teach others His Word?)

_____

_____

_____

_____

DO IT UP

If you're serious about learning more about God's Word, you'll need an action plan. Here is one to follow:

STEP ONE: Plan!

What steps will you take this week to learn more about God's Word? Who might you connect with to help you? Put some thought into your response. Don't give some vague, off-the-top-of-your-head answer. Be specific. What exactly are you planning to do? When will you do it?

STEP TWO: Act!

Put your plan into action and then answer these questions. Did things go as you thought they would? Was it easier or harder than you expected to talk to people about it? Did you find what you were looking for?

STEP THREE: Review!

How thoroughly did you plan your steps? Are you satisfied with the way things turned about? Would you do anything differently, if you could?

LITTLE BIBLE BACKGROUND

Link 2

Address the question that your group members may be thinking, but may not have the ability to phrase: **If Jesus was God, and God gave the Bible, why did Jesus need to learn about it from human teachers?** Point out that when Jesus came to earth, He willingly volunteered to live as a human (Phil. 2:6-8). While He remained God, He mysteriously also underwent the normal process of human development. Therefore, it was necessary for Him to learn about Scripture like everyone else—though it does appear that He was unusually advanced for His age.

Link 3

Needed: Index cards

Before you wrap up the session, hand out index cards. Ask your group members to write down three questions they have about the Bible or the Christian life, questions that they would like to answer. Direct them to specific passages, reference books, or people who can help the students.

ADVANCED LEARNERS

Link 1

After your group members finish Resource 1A, spend a few minutes talking about their earliest Christian learning experiences. Use the following questions to guide your discussion: **What were some of the first things you remember learning about God? about Jesus? about God's Word? about sin and salvation? Who helped you understand these things at an early age? How did their teaching affect the way you learn today?**

Link 3

Put your advanced learners on the spot with this question: **Have you ever considered teaching others about the Christian life or God's Word?** Spend a few minutes talking about any reluctance on your group members' part to assume a role of responsibility.

MOSTLY GUYS

Link 1

Focus your discussion on skills that in today's society are usually associated with guys—things that are necessary to know in order to avoid having one's manhood questioned. These skills may include anything from playing sports to shooting a gun to having sex. You might even ask: **What are the five most important things for a guy to know?** From there, you can talk about the five most important things for a Christian to know—and how they can learn those things.

Link 3

Ask the guys to think of a verse or passage in the Bible that they already know. With their accountability partners, have them talk about how God has used that verse or passage to help, comfort, or sustain them during trying times. Have them pray together and talk about the steps they will take this week to learn God's Word.

MOSTLY GIRLS

Link 1

Focus your discussion on some of the "private" things that girls have to learn about—things like menstruation, reproduction, birth control, etc. Ask volunteers to talk about their experiences in learning about such things. Who taught them? How awkward was the situation? Use the discussion to introduce the idea of Christian teachers.

Link 3

Ask the girls to get with their accountability partners. Have each student think of a verse or story from the Bible that has inspired or helped her during a specific time in her life. Have them pray together and talk about the steps they will take this week to learn God's Word.

MEDIA

Link 1

Needed: Instructional videotapes

Raid your church's video library for all kinds of instructional tapes dealing with various aspects of the Christian life. Show brief segments of several different tapes, and let group members comment on what they like or don't like about each tape or instructor. Use this activity to lead into a discussion of the type of teacher your group members prefer.

Link 3

Needed: Video camera, tape, player and TV

Set up a "video-teaching service." Ask your students to examine a portion of Scripture and prepare a quick, two- to three-minute devotion on what the passage means to him or her. Allow the students to do this individually or in pairs. Film each student or pair as they give their devotional to the group.

EXTRA ADRENALINE

Link 1

Needed: Golf instructor, golf clubs and golf balls

Bring in a golf instructor (or at least someone you know who knows the game pretty well). Ask him to teach your students the basics of swinging a club. Let students try hitting a ball a few times without instruction and then a few times after receiving instruction. See what kind of difference the teaching makes. Use the activity to lead into a discussion of the difference instruction can make in the lives of young Christians.

Link 2

Ask a couple of volunteers to act out a scene in which confused disciples try to interpret one of Jesus' parables without His guidance. The weirder the interpretation the disciples come up with, the funnier the skit will be.

JUNIOR HIGH

Link 1

Here's a fun twist for your junior highers: ask them to get up in front of the group and give instructions for things they know nothing about. Let them "teach" the rest of the group about things like driving, getting into college, buying a house, or living alone. Encourage them to try to sound as convincing as possible.

Link 3

Ask: **What do you think makes a good student?** Let your group members throw out some suggestions like paying attention to teachers, having good study habits, and wanting to learn. Point out that if they want to be taught about God's Word or the Christian life, they need to be good students.

Planning Checklist

LINK 1: Avid Learners

❑ Advanced Learners
❑ Mostly Guys
❑ Mostly Girls
❑ Media
❑ Extra Adrenaline
❑ Junior High

LINK 2: Jesus Learned Too!

❑ Little Bible Background
❑ Extra Adrenaline

LINK 3: Ideal Candidates

❑ Little Bible Background
❑ Advanced Learners
❑ Mostly Guys
❑ Mostly Girls
❑ Media
❑ Junior High

2
MEMORABLE
WORDS

KEY QUESTIONS

- What does it mean to "hide" God's Word in our hearts?
- What example did Jesus set for memorizing Scripture and using it at just the right moment?
- What steps can you take to hide God's Word in your heart?

BIBLE BASE

Deuteronomy 6:13, 16; 8:3;
Psalms 91:11-12; 119:11;
Matthew 4:1-11

SUPPLIES

- Paper
- 10 household items (Opener)
- Copies of Resources 2A, 2B, Journal
- Pencils
- Bibles

Opener (Optional)

Don't you forget about things

Needed: 10 household items

This game will work well as an opening activity for this session on memorization. Line up 10 common household items behind you so the students can't see them. Bring them out one at a time and show them to the students for 10 seconds. After you have shown each item to the group, hand out the paper and pencils and ask them to write down what they saw. After the students have finished making their lists, go over their answers. Ask them what was hard or easy about the game. Ask the student who remembered the most items how he or she did it.

LEARNER LINK

Memorization has gotten a bad wrap of late. Often your students are reduced to mindless automatons, mumbling words by rote to prove they can memorize God's Word. Your challenge is to get God's Word from short-term memory, forgotten as the students walk out your door, to long-term memory. As you discuss this opener, point out to the students how easy it is to forget things, even the things held in front of their faces for 10 seconds! Ask students if they have any studying or memorizing tricks to help the words go deeper.

You can make the transition from the game to the session by saying something like this: **You guys were pretty good at remembering what the objects were. How good are you at remembering other things?**

Link 1

MAKING IT REAL

Introduce your group members to the art of journaling. Ask your students to keep a journal or diary of their observations, feelings, and frustrations as they take steps each day to be a more devoted disciple of Jesus Christ. Encourage them to be consistent in writing in their journals. Point out that journaling may be difficult at first, but that the more they do it, the better they will become. Furthermore, the better they become, the more they will benefit from it.

A Test of Memory

If you handed out Resource 1C at the end of Session 1, take a few minutes at the beginning of this meeting to find out how well your students did at locating potential mentors. Ask volunteers to share their experiences, both positive and negative, with the rest of the group. Encourage other group members to offer their comments on the volunteers' experiences. Emphasize that you're looking for generous praise and constructive criticism. Your group members should feel comfortable enough with each other to be open and honest about their struggles and successes.

Introduce the session this way: **Today we're going to be talking about memory. But before we get into our discussion, I want to take a few minutes to check your memory banks and see what's up there. To do that, I'm going to run a little test. I'll start a sentence or a phrase, and you finish it.**

Below you'll find a list of commercial jingles and Bible verses. By the time you use this material, some, if not all, of the jingles may be outdated. If so, you'll need to substitute a list of current popular jingles and catch phrases. The Bible verses will still be timely.

- Yo quiero . . . (Taco Bell.)
- In the beginning . . . (God created the heavens and the earth.)
- Visa—it's everywhere . . . (you want to be.)
- Ask and it will be given to you; seek and you will find . . . (knock and the door will be opened to you.)
- Be all that you . . . (can be.)
- For the wages of sin is death . . . (but the gift of God is eternal life in Christ Jesus our Lord.)
- Now faith is being sure of what we hope for and certain of . . . (what we do not see.)
- Did somebody say . . . (McDonald's?)
- And now these three remain: faith, hope and love. . . . (But the greatest of these is love.)

The almost inevitable result of this activity is that your students will be able to recall more jingles than Bible verses. (If anyone complains that the Bible verses you read were too obscure, challenge that person to recite as many other passages as possible. See if the person rises to or shrinks from the challenge.) Use the following questions and suggestions to guide your discussion of the activity:

- **How do you feel knowing that you're more familiar with commercials than Bible verses?** Some students may be a little embarrassed; others won't see what the big deal is. **Why do you suppose that is? Do you spend time memorizing commercials?** (The primary culprit is the ever-present television. The more we hear something, the more likely it is that we'll remember it. Sometimes we absorb knowledge, like the lyrics to jingles and catchy slogans, without even knowing it.)

How many Scripture passages would you say you know by heart? Encourage volunteers to share, if they're comfortable with it. The last thing you want to do is put someone on the spot here or make one of your group members feel like a heathen for not knowing more Bible verses.

Why is it important to memorize Scripture? Emphasize that you're not looking for "churchy" answers here. You want to know whether your group members honestly see a need in their lives for memorizing Bible passages.

What are some problems you face in trying to memorize Bible passages? (One problem is knowing what to memorize. How are we supposed to choose from the thousands of verses in the Bible? Another problem is the old-fashioned language of the Bible. It's hard to memorize words and phrases that aren't part of our own vocabulary.)

Introduce the Bible study portion of your meeting this way: **Let's take a look at an incident in Jesus' life where knowing Scripture passages by heart proved to be life-saving.**

The Power of Words

Hand out copies of "Sticks and Stones May Break My Bones, but Words Will Chase the Devil Away" (Resource 2A). Explain: This is the story of Jesus' temptation by Satan. Most of the details have already been filled in—everything except Jesus' words. Look up the story in Matthew 4:1-11 and write down Jesus' three responses to the devil.

After a few minutes, ask group members to share what they wrote down. The correct answers are as follows:

- "It is written: 'Man does not live by bread alone, but on every word that comes from the mouth of God.'"
- "It is also written: 'Do not put the Lord your God to the test.'"
- "Away from me, Satan! For it is written: 'Worship the Lord your God, and serve him only.'"

Before you get into a discussion about Jesus' responses, briefly review the circumstances of His temptation.

What condition was Jesus in when Satan appeared to Him in the desert? (He hadn't eaten for 40 days, so He was probably extremely weak.)

Why do you suppose Satan chose that time to tempt Jesus? (Satan probably saw Jesus as being vulnerable in His weakened condition.)

What do you notice about the words Jesus used to resist the devil's temptations? Your group members will probably mention that all of Jesus' responses were preceded by the phrase, "It is written." Jesus defended Himself by quoting Scripture. What your group members may not recognize is that Jesus seemed to know the exact words to use to deflect the power of Satan's temptation.

How do you think Jesus was able to quote such pertinent verses that made His point in such an intense situation? (He spent much time studying Scripture and meditating on Scripture. He turned it over again and again in His mind so that it was fresh. He loved God and God's Word intensely. His relationship with God was very close. He depended on God and listened to Him.)

Ask one of your group members to read aloud three passages from the fifth book of the Bible: Deuteronomy 8:3; 6:16; and 6:13. Ask: **What do these verses have in common?** (These are the passages Jesus quoted to Satan.)
Ask another group member to read aloud Psalm 91:11-12. Discuss: **What's the significance of this verse?** (This is the passage Satan quoted to Jesus. Even the devil recognized the power of memorizing Scripture!)

Finally, have one of your group members read Psalm 119:11. Ask: **Do you think this verse still applies today? Can hiding God's Word in our heart—memorizing it—knowing it—keep us from doing the wrong things? Can knowing Scripture lead us into a deeper and closer relationship with God?** Get a few responses before moving on to Step 3.

An Ounce of Prevention

Hold up your Bible for everyone to see. Point out: **People in ancient times didn't have access to personal Bibles like we do. For them, memorization was a necessary part of life. Most of us, on the other hand, have access to as many Bibles as we need. If you've ever been in a Christian bookstore, you know that you can find** *hundreds* **of different versions and translations of God's Word. You can walk into most hotel rooms in this country and find a Bible. Since we have the Bible literally at our fingertips, do we really have to memorize passages? Can't we just look them up when we need them?** It should be interesting to hear your group members' opinions on this subject.

To help your group members understand that memorizing God's Word is still an important part of a disciple's life, ask them to participate in a brief demonstration.

Explain: **I'm going to describe a life-threatening situation, and I want you to demonstrate what you would do in that situation, based on what you've been taught. For example, let's say there's a fire in the building and it's spreading fast. What would you do?** Your group members should drop to the floor and crawl to the nearest exit, in order to avoid smoke inhalation. When they get to the door, they should touch it to see if it's hot before opening it.

While your group members are crawling on the floor, say: **Oh, no! A part of the ceiling collapsed and one of the flames set your clothes on fire! What should you do?** Your group members should roll around on the ground to smother the flames.

Okay, it turns out that there's not a fire in the building, but there is a tornado heading right at us. What would you do? Your group members should move away from any windows and go to the basement or the lowest part of the building.

No, that rumbling we heard isn't an oncoming tornado—it's an earthquake! What would you do? Your group members should position themselves in the doorframe of the room.

After you've had some fun with this activity, ask: **How did you know what to do in all of these situations?** Chances are, your students have heard those things so many times at home and at school that they're almost like second nature.

What if, during a fire or a tornado or an earthquake, you had to stop and look up instructions on what to do? (Unfortunately, by the time you find the information you need, it may be too late.)

How might we apply this same principle to memorizing Scripture? (It's true that our access to Bibles makes it easier for us to find verses. But sometimes, in an emergency, we won't have time to go to the Bible and flip through a concordance. We need words of wisdom that are on the tip of our tongue and in the depths of our heart.)

What kind of emergency situations might call for immediate Bible recall? (Temptation, especially sexual temptation, can take root very quickly. If we don't counterattack immediately with a word of wisdom, we may find ourselves giving in. Likewise, if we encounter someone in need of immediate comfort and assurance, it would be more than a little awkward to make the person wait while we fumble around looking for the right thing to say from God's Word.)

Hand out copies of "Memory Starters" (Resource 2B). Explain: **On this sheet you'll find several different situations and circumstances that call for comfort or direction from God's Word. Rather than taking the time to look up these passages every time you need them, wouldn't it be better to memorize them so that they're always available to you?** Encourage comments from your group members.

If you have some extra time at the end of your meeting, pair your group members up for some sharing about what the Bible verses on Resource 2B mean to them. Point out that it isn't enough just to memorize Scripture—even a computer can hold the words in its heart (its hard drive)! So give students the opportunity to choose at least one passage and tell each other: (1) how I understand the verse, and (2) what it means to me in my daily life. Be sure to provide plenty of praise and encouragement as your group members take an important step toward understanding God's Word more fully.

There are so many different levels and intricacies to our relationship with God. Scripture memory really isn't as on the surface as it might seem. Knowing Scripture is a work of your heart, your head, your experience, and your spirit. Be sure to take all of these aspects into account as you take steps to commit God's Word to memory.

LEARNER LINK

Challenge the accountability partners to help each other memorize as many verses in the next week as possible. In your next meeting, set aside some time to see which pair learned the most verses.

MAKING IT REAL

Some of your students may have needs that don't get addressed during your group time. Make a special effort to get to know all of your students individually. That may mean a phone call or a trip to a sporting event or a lunch together. Not only will this help you build relationships with the students, but seeing you outside of your discipleship group will help them connect what they learn to their everyday lives.

As you conclude the session, hand out copies of the student journal "Heart Check: A Practical Approach to Hiding God's Word in Your Heart" (Resource 2C). The sheet is intended to motivate each group member to commit one Bible passage to memory this week.

Then have your students get together with their accountability partners and share their plans. They should commit to praying for each other this week concerning the plans they just made. Also have students pray together now or bring them back to a large group and pray for the commitments they just made. Encourage your students to set aside a few minutes each day to work on the sheet and follow through on their "action plans."

Sticks and Stones May Break My Bones, but Words Will Chase the Devil Away

The Temptation of Jesus

Then Jesus was led by the Spirit into the desert to be tempted by the devil. After fasting forty days and forty nights, he was hungry. The Tempter came to him and said, "If you are the Son of God, tell these stones to become bread."

Images by ©PhotoDisc, Inc.

JESUS ANSWERED,

Then the devil took him to the holy city and had him stand on the highest point of the temple. "If you are the Son of God," he said, "throw yourself down. For it is written: 'He will command his angels concerning you, and they will lift you up in their hands, so that you will not strike your foot against a stone.'"

JESUS ANSWERED HIM,

Again, the devil took him to a very high mountain and showed him all the kingdoms of the world and their splendor. "All this I will give you," he said, "if you will bow down and worship me."

JESUS SAID TO HIM,

Then the devil left him, and angels came and attended him.

Memory Starters

There are many great verses in the Bible to hide in your heart. Where should you begin? Depends on what you're looking for. Below are a list of subjects and verses that apply to them. Decide which ones apply to you or the people you know and start with those verses.

CONFLICT
"We love because he first loved us. If anyone says, 'I love God,' yet hates his brother, he is a liar. For anyone who does not love his brother, whom he has seen, cannot love God, whom he has not seen. And he has given us this command: Whoever loves God must also love his brother" (1 John 4:19-21).

DISCOURAGEMENT
"Blessed is the man who perseveres under trial, because when he has stood the test, he will receive the crown of life that God has promised to those who love him" (James 1:12).

DOUBT
"But I will trust in your unfailing love; my heart rejoices in your salvation. I will sing to the LORD, for he has been good to me" (Ps. 13:5-6).

GUILT
"If we confess our sins, he is faithful and just and will forgive us our sins and purify us from all unrighteousness" (1 John 1:9).

TEMPTATION
"Submit yourselves, then, to God. Resist the devil and he will flee from you" (James 4:7).

WORRY
"Cast all you anxiety on him, for he cares for you." (1 Peter 5:7)

HEART CHECK:
A Practical Approach to Hiding God's Word in Your Heart

You may think you've picked up some valuable tips for memorizing God's Word, but unless you actually put those tips to use in your life, they're useless. Remember, God wants not only "listeners" of His Word, but "doers" (James 1:22). This sheet is for doers.

LOOK IT UP

Below you'll find seven Scripture references, one for every day of the week. Each passage listed below has something interesting to say about hiding God's Word in your heart. Spend a few minutes each day looking up the passage and writing down a few (relevant) ideas that pop into your head.

DAY ONE: Deuteronomy 6:6-9 (What kind of regular reminders might assist us in memorizing God's Word?)

_____
_____
_____
_____

DAY TWO: Isaiah 48:17-18 (How does memorizing God's Word help us pay attention to His commands?)

_____
_____
_____
_____

DAY THREE: Proverbs 3:3 (How can memorizing God's Word help us keep love and faithfulness as important parts of our lives?)

_____
_____
_____
_____

DAY FOUR: Psalm 143:5 (Why do you think it's important for us to remember what the Lord has done?)

_____
_____
_____

☺ TALK IT UP

Jesus assures us that "all things are possible with God" (Mark 10:27). That includes memorizing Scripture. So when you're faced with an obstacle that interferes with your commitment to hiding God's Word in your heart, a wise first step is to talk to God about it. Take some time to write down a few prayer requests, specific ways in which you need the Lord to help you focus on His Word. (For example, you might ask Him to help you recall verses when you need them.) Don't be afraid to get personal here. No one else needs to see your request list.

_____
_____
_____
_____
_____
_____
_____
_____
_____
_____
_____
_____
_____
_____
_____
_____
_____
_____

DAY FIVE: Isaiah 55:10-11 (What does this passage tell us about the value of God's Word?)

_____
_____
_____
_____

DAY SIX: Amos 8:11-12 (What do you think our society would be like if God were to send this kind of famine today?)

_____
_____
_____
_____

DAY SEVEN: Colossians 3:16 (What does it mean to let the Word of God "dwell" in us "richly"?)

_____
_____
_____
_____

DO IT UP

If you're serious about memorizing Scripture, you'll need an action plan. Here is one to follow:

STEP ONE: Plan!

What steps will you take this week to memorize a passage of Scripture? Put some thought into your response. Be specific. What exactly are you planning to do? When will you do it? How much time will you set aside?

STEP TWO: Act!

Put your plan into action and then answer these questions. How did it go? Was it easier or harder than you expected? What was the most difficult part of the process?

STEP THREE: Review!

What good do you think the passage you memorized will do you? Do you feel any different toward God's Word? Do you think you'll make this a habit in your life?

LITTLE BIBLE BACKGROUND

Link 2

Ask: **Do you think it would be possible to make God's Word as much a part of your everyday life as television? Why or why not?** If your group members don't totally dismiss the idea, spend a few minutes coming up with some practical ideas for increasing our everyday exposure to God's Word. Ask them how much Scripture they might be able to memorize if it was that prevalent in their lives.

Link 3

If your group members are a little skittish about trying to memorize Bible verses, introduce the idea of mnemonics, using things like formulas, rhymes, and mental pictures to help with the memorization process. An example of a mnemonic device involves the order of the planets in the solar system. Instead of memorizing Mercury, Venus, Earth, Mars, Jupiter, Saturn, Uranus, Neptune, and Pluto, some people prefer to remember it this way:" My very excellent mother just served us nine pizzas." Note that each word in the sentence begins with the same letter as its corresponding planet. As a group, develop a similar strategy for memorizing one of the passages on Resource 2B.

ADVANCED LEARNERS

Link 2

Demonstrate the point that we need to have Bible verses stored away in our memory because trying to find relevant verses in the Bible can be time-consuming. Divide the group into pairs, making sure that each pair has a Bible. Explain that you will call out a topic and point to a pair. The two group members will then have exactly one minute to find a verse that deals with that topic. See how well your advanced learners do when it comes time to put their knowledge to use.

Link 3

Ask: **How many of you know what a phylactery** [fih-LACK-tuh-ree] **is?** If no one knows, ask someone to read Matthew 23:5. Explain that phylacteries were small boxes that contained Bible passages. Ancient Israelites wore these on their foreheads and arms to keep God's Word before them at all times. Discuss some things that we could use as modern phylacteries, ideas for keeping God's Word in our minds.

MOSTLY GUYS

Link 1

Introduce the topic of memory by discussing the differences between the things a guy is likely to remember and the things a girl is likely to remember. Ask: **Have you ever gotten in trouble with your girlfriend because you forgot something like the anniversary of your first kiss? Why do you think many girls consider things like that important? Why do you think many guys consider things like that unimportant?** Introduce the topic of your session by trying to find "common ground," things that both guys and girls think are important enough to remember. One suggestion, could be Bible passages.

Link 3

Suggest one more Bible verse for your group members to memorize, one that describes the ideal maturation process for a young man. Because it's relatively short, it would be a good candidate for your group members' first memorization project. The verse is Luke 2:52: "And Jesus grew in wisdom and stature, and in favor with God and men."

MOSTLY GIRLS

Link 1

Discuss as a group the kinds of things girls remember, as opposed to the kinds of things guys remember. Use the following questions to guide your discussion:

• Do you know the birthdates of your best friends? Do you think guys know the birthdates of their best friends?

• Do you remember what your friend bought you for Christmas or your last birthday? Do you think he remembers what you bought him?

• Do you remember the first movie you and your friend and/or boyfriend saw together? Do you think he remembers?

Introduce the session topic by trying to find "common ground," things that both guys and girls think are important enough to remember—including, Bible passages.

Link 3

Suggest one more passage for your girls to memorize, one that concludes the Book of Proverbs' description of "the wife of noble character." The passage is Proverbs 31:29-31: "Many women do noble things, but you surpass them all. Charm is deceptive, and beauty is fleeting; but a woman who fears the LORD is to be praised. Give her the reward she has earned, and let her works bring her praise at the city gate."

MEDIA

Link 1

Needed: Videotape of commercials, video player and TV

Play "Name that Commercial." Before the meeting, you'll need to record several minutes' worth of commercials. Make sure you get a sampling from several different networks. (Also make sure that you screen the commercials you record to make sure that you avoid any objectionable material.) Ask the students to raise their hands as soon as they think they know what the commercial is. Pause the tape to give him or her a chance to guess. See who guesses the most commercials correctly.

Link 3

Needed: Recording of songs and a tape or CD player

Bring in tapes of several songs that are based on Bible passages—songs like "Thy Word," which is based on Psalm 119:105 or even "Turn, Turn, Turn" by The Byrds, which is based on Ecclesiastes 3:1-8. As you play the songs for your group members, point out that such tunes could be great memory aids for helping them hide God's Word in their heart. Briefly discuss as a group why songs are so much easier to remember than printed material.

EXTRA ADRENALINE

Opener

For a more active opener, try a game called "What's Different?" You will send one person out of the room. While he's gone, the rest of the group will change one thing in the room. For example, one person might sit in a different seat or remove one of her shoes. The change should be something apparent, but not obvious. When the person returns, he has to figure out what is different. Take turns sending people out of the room until everyone has had a chance to be the contestant.

Link 3

Think of some people that your students are familiar with and write their names on slips of paper. Use a variety of people some that your students know well and some they only really know about. For example: Michael Jordan, your mom, your best friend, Elizabeth Dole, the principal of your school. Then put each slip of paper in a different balloon and blow it up. Have some balloons with names and some without names. After students pop the balloons by sitting on them they should try to describe the person who is on the slip of paper they got out of the balloon. Point out how different it is to know about someone and to actually know someone.

JUNIOR HIGH

Link 1
Kick off your discussion with this question: How many things does a person your age have to have memorized to get through a normal day? This is a tough question, so you may need to walk your students through a typical day to see how often they rely on their memories. You can get as specific as you'd like, pointing out that memory is necessary for everything from remembering how to turn off your alarm clock in the morning to remembering where you live in order to get home after school. Discuss how easy or difficult it would be to add other things like Bible passages to our current memory load.

Link 2
Add one more Bible passage to your study: Luke 2:41-52. Ask: **What do we learn about Jesus from this passage?** (His Bible knowledge wasn't something He developed just as an adult; it was something He began before He was even a teenager.) **What does this passage say to students who think they're too young to get seriously involved in the Bible?** (Jesus' example proves that people of all ages have a responsibility to know God's Word.)

Planning Checklist

OPENER: Don't You Forget about Things
❏ Extra Adrenaline

LINK 1: A Test of Memory
❏ Mostly Guys
❏ Mostly Girls
❏ Media
❏ Junior High

LINK 2: The Power of Words
❏ Little Bible Background
❏ Advanced Learners
❏ Junior High

LINK 3: An Ounce of Prevention
❏ Little Bible Background
❏ Advanced Learners
❏ Mostly Guys
❏ Mostly Girls
❏ Media
❏ Extra Adrenaline

MAKE NO MISTAKE

KEY QUESTIONS

- What happens if we misunderstand what the Bible is saying to us?
- What did Jesus say about the importance of understanding God's Word?
- How did Jesus exemplify ways to be sure we're correctly understanding God's Word?

BIBLE BASE

John 16:15-17
Ephesians 4:11-16
Matthew 5:38-39

SUPPLIES

- Paper
- Bibles
- Chalkboard and chalk or newsprint and markers
- Pencils
- Copies of Resources 3A, 3B, Journal

Opener (Optional)

Mixed Messages

Start things off by giving everyone a piece of paper and a pencil. Hand a Bible to one of your group members and ask him to read James 1:19-25 to himself very carefully. When he's done, take the Bible away, and ask him to write the passage—or at least as much of it as he can remember—on his sheet of paper. If he can't remember the exact words of the passage, he should at least write down the general point.

When the person is finished writing, hand his sheet of paper to the next person in the room. Give her a moment to read what the first person wrote, then take the sheet away and ask her to write what she can remember of it, whether it's exact words or a general approximation. Continue until everyone gets a chance to write something down.

Collect the last sheet of paper, read what's written on it, then ask someone else to read aloud James 1:19-25. Compare the two versions to see how well your group members interpreted and passed along the message.

Use the following questions to guide your discussion of the activity:
- **What happened with your version of the passage? Why is it different?**
- **What are some of the important parts of this passage that your version left out?**
- **Overall, do you think your version is good enough to help someone who doesn't know much about the Bible understand James 1:19-25?**

Introduce the session topic this way: **Today we're going to be talking about how important it is to really understand what the Bible says.**

LEARNER LINK

This may seem a lot like the game "Telephone." That's because it is. We all know how difficult it is to really understand what somebody first said, when we get second- or third-hand or worse! If possible, remind the students that it's important to learn the Bible for themselves, instead of just relying solely on what other people say about it.

MAKING IT REAL

As you get to know your students better, pray for them specifically. Taking the time to do this will help you focus on their needs. It will also help you to continually acknowledge and trust that it is God who is making these students into disciples of Jesus Christ—sometimes even in spite of your efforts!

Link 1

THERE MUST BE SOME MISUNDERSTANDING

If you handed out Resource 2C at the end of Session 2, take a few minutes at the beginning of this meeting to find out how well your students did at memorizing Scripture passages last week. Ask if any partners learned verses together and ask them to recite the verses they learned.

Begin this session by questioning your group members about their musical listening habits. In order to answer, your students may have to reveal some harmlessly embarrassing information about themselves. That's why it's important that you keep the atmosphere non-threatening and fun. Don't be afraid to chime in with your own responses along the way. Here are some questions you can use:

How much time do you spend listening to music every day, whether it's in your car, in your room, or anywhere else? You might ask group members to estimate the number of songs they hear every day.

How often do you sing along when you listen? Do you usually try to disguise it when you sing or are you pretty obvious about it? Ask a couple of your group members to share stories of getting "caught" singing in the car by another driver. **Do you ever try to sing along with songs even though you don't know the words?** Ask volunteers to share their secrets for faking it.

Have you ever had one of those situations where somebody heard you sing the wrong words to a song and made you feel like an idiot? Encourage a brave soul or two to share their experiences. Name some lyrics that you used to sing wrong before you found out how they really went. Make the point that misunderstanding a song lyric is no big deal. The worst thing that could happen is that you embarrass yourself a little. There are some things, however, that should never be misunderstood.

Ask your group members to make a list of things that must be understood correctly. The list might include things like landing coordinates from an airport control tower, X-rays a surgeon uses as a guide while performing surgery, and instructions for life-saving techniques such as CPR. If no one mentions it, suggest that the Bible is also something that must be understood correctly—and Jesus helps us do it.

Link 2

JESUS CLEARS IT UP

Start your Bible study with a few questions to get your students thinking: **How hard is it to understand what the Bible is saying?** Ask your group members to identify specific things about the Bible that are difficult to understand.

Is it possible to truly understand what the Bible is saying just from reading it? If your students are confused by the question, point out that some people go to school for years, studying ancient languages, archaeology, world history, and other subjects, just to be able to understand the Bible better.

Is there anything Jesus did that helps us understand God's Word better—things that don't involve four years of college? Get a few responses. Then form three groups and have each small group study one of these Scripture passages:

John 16:15-17
Ephesians 4:11-16
Matthew 5:38-39 (compared with Exodus 21:24)

Tell students that their task is to study the passage as though they had to explain it to someone else like a little brother or sister or a good friend. They'll do it by working together to complete this simple outline (jot it on the chalkboard or newsprint, if possible)—

Title:
The Big, Main Point:
Some Other Points to Make:
A Real-life Application:

Let group members know that they can highlight any particular portion of the Bible passages they've discussed. Tell your students that the challenge is to make their presentation as clear as possible. After a few minutes, ask volunteers to tell about their Bible passages and express the key point they would want to stress. Make sure that these three points come through as ways that Jesus helps us understand God's Word:

Point #1: Jesus provides us the "Spirit of truth" (NIV) who will live within us always. (John 16:15-17)
Point #2: Jesus gives us prophets, pastors, and teachers to teach us the truth and to protect us from deceitful teachers and false teachings. (Eph. 4:11-16)
Point #3: Jesus gives us His example of using context to interpret the Scriptures. (Matt. 5:38-39)

Now help your students understand more fully what it means to find the context of a Bible passage. Give them an exercise designed to help them understand the concept of context a little better. Distribute copies of "It's All in the Context" (Resource 3A).

Explain: **This sheet contains ten simple phrases that you might hear on any given day. These phrases may seem straightforward and obvious, but actually they could have several different meanings and interpretations, depending on who's speaking or what the circumstances are. I want you to imagine a scenario for each phrase that would help put its meaning in context.** Give students a few minutes to work on the sheet. When everyone is finished, ask volunteers to share their answers.

After group members have shared their interpretations, ask: **How dangerous would you say it is to read the Bible without knowing the context of what you're reading?** If no one mentions it, point out that for thousands of years people have been using the Bible to justify everything from war to slavery. That's the kind of abuse that can result from not understanding what God's Word is really saying.

Link 3

FOR DEMONSTRATION PURPOSES ONLY

Now point out that there are other places in Scripture—in addition to Jesus' words and example—that help us know how to interpret the Word correctly. Hand out copies of "Five Steps to Understanding the Bible" (Resource 3B). Point out that the five "study tips" are simple enough to be used by anyone. Let your group members work in pairs to complete the sheet, then discuss their answers.

To practice these five steps, have someone read Luke 14:26. Then ask: **What might happen if a person misunderstood this verse?** If no one mentions this, point out to your group that some cults base their religious philosophy on this passage. These cults forbid their members from ever having contact with their families. Obviously this is an extreme example, but there is tremendous potential for pain, misery, and broken family relationships if we misunderstand what Jesus is saying here. As a group, work through the five steps. If needed, supplement the discussion with the answers below.

Step One: You might ask Him to prevent you from doing anything rash, as far as your family is concerned, while you work to figure out what this verse is really saying.

Step Two: The verse before it tells us that Jesus was talking to the large crowds of people who were following Him. The verses that follow it talk about personal sacrifice and counting the cost before making a big decision.)

Step Three: If your group members need help, give them a concordance or topical index to search through. Among other references, they may find that the fifth commandment in Exodus 20:12 instructs us to "honor" our father and mother. Ephesians 5:22–6:4 gives us all kinds of instructions about loving our spouses and children and obeying our parents.

Step Four: Suggest to your students that a mature Christian would probably explain Luke 14:26 this way: **Jesus wanted those who were tagging along with Him to know that He required complete commitment from His disciples. If a person makes a decision to follow Jesus, everything else in that person's life— including his family—must take a back-seat to the Lord. The love we have for Jesus should be so intense that it makes all other forms of love—including family love—seem like hate.**

Step Five: If you think your students might be uncomfortable sharing their responses with the rest of the group, let them silently reflect on them for a minute or two.

LEARNER **LINK**

Divide your group up into accountability partners. Have them work together either to memorize the five-step process that they have been going over or give them another passage of Scripture to work on. If you know specific passages students have questioned in the past, suggest that they take the five steps and go through the passage together. Be sure to walk around the room to offer any needed assistance.

As you wrap up the session, distribute copies of the student journal "Heart Check: A Practical Approach to Understanding God's Word" (Resource 3C). The sheet is designed to motivate each group member to study the Bible more intently in the coming week. Have students spend some time in class answering the questions under the "Plan!" section of "Do It Up"—the last part of the worksheet.

MAKING IT R E A L

A big part of discipleship is encouraging your students to put what they have learned into action. As their leader, you should be constantly looking for teachable moments—times when you are together with the students, outside of your group time, in which you can encourage them to practice what they have been learning. Another great way to do this is to set up service projects or experiential learning times. Session five in this book provides what you need to set up one of these learning experiences.

Then have your students get together with their accountability partners and share their plans. They should commit to praying for each other this week concerning the plans they just made. Also have students pray together now or bring them back to a large group and pray for the commitments they just made. Encourage your students to set aside a few minutes each day to work on the sheet and follow through on their "action plans."

It's All in the Context

The following phrases may seem simple enough. But depending on who's talking and what the circumstances are, they could actually have several totally different meanings. Below each statement, describe who you picture saying it and how you picture it being said.

Take the sentence, "She has a great personality," for example. If it's spoken by a beauty pageant judge, it has one meaning. If it's spoken by someone trying to set up a blind date, it has another meaning. It's all a matter of context.

1. "THIS IS THE WRONG CAR."

2. "IT'S PAYBACK TIME."

3. "I THINK WE'RE IN TROUBLE."

4. "HE'S GOING TO DIE."

© PhotoDisc, Inc.

5. "I KNOW JUST HOW YOU FEEL."

6. "I GIVE UP."

7. "SHE HAS A GREAT PERSONALITY."

8. "THIS TIME IT'S PERSONAL."

9. "I CAN'T BELIEVE YOU JUST DID THAT."

10. "DO YOU WANT TO WALK OUT OF HERE OR DO YOU WANT TO BE CARRIED OUT?"

© PhotoDisc, Inc.

Five Steps to Understanding the Bible

Each of the passages listed below has something important to say about how to understand the Bible. Your job is to look up each one and write down what it says about understanding the Bible.

STEP ONE
Pray for the Holy Spirit's guidance.
1 Corinthians 2:12-16

STEP TWO
Put the passage into its proper context.
2 Timothy 2:15

STEP THREE
Compare it with what you know
about other passages of Scripture.
2 Timothy 3:16

STEP FOUR
Get input from mature Christians.
Proverbs 9:9; 15:22

STEP FIVE
Apply the wisdom of the passage to your life.
James 1:22-25

HEART CHECK:
A Practical Approach to Understanding God's Word

You may think you've picked up some valuable tips for understanding God's Word, but unless you actually put them to use in your life these tips are worthless. Remember, God wants not only "listeners" of His Word, but "doers" (James 1:22). This sheet is for doers.

LOOK IT UP

Below you'll find seven Scripture references, one for every day of the week. Each passage listed below has something interesting to say about understanding the Bible. Spend a few minutes each day looking up the passage and writing down a few (relevant) thoughts that pop into your head.

DAY ONE: Joshua 1:8 (How does meditating on God's Word help us understand it?)

_____
_____
_____
_____

DAY TWO: Psalm 119:11 (How does memorizing or "hiding" God's Word in our hearts help us understand it?)

_____
_____
_____
_____

DAY THREE: Ephesians 6:17 (Why is it important for us to understand God's Word?)

_____
_____
_____
_____

DAY FOUR: John 15:7 (What does it mean that God's Words "remain" in us?)

_____
_____
_____
_____

☺ TALK IT UP

Jesus tells us that "all things are possible with God" (Mark 10:27). That includes understanding His Word as He meant it to be understood. So when you're faced with a passage that doesn't make sense to you, a wise first step is to consult the One who makes all things possible. Take some time to write down a few prayer requests, specific ways in which you need the Lord to help you approach Scripture. (For example, you might ask Him to help you find the context of the passages you study.) Don't be afraid to get personal here. No one else needs to see your prayer request list.

_____
_____
_____
_____
_____
_____
_____
_____
_____
_____
_____
_____
_____
_____
_____
_____
_____

DAY FIVE: 2 Timothy 3:16-17 (How is God's Word useful in "correcting" us?)

_____
_____
_____
_____

DAY SIX: Matthew 13:10 (What did the disciples do when they couldn't understand what Jesus was saying?)

_____
_____
_____
_____

DAY SEVEN: Matthew 13:11-17 (What kind of people understand Jesus' parables?)

_____
_____
_____
_____

DO IT UP

If you're serious about understanding the Bible as Jesus intended for us, you'll need an action plan. Here is one to follow:

STEP ONE: Plan!

What steps will you take this week to make sure that you understand the Bible passages you study? Put some thought into your response. Be specific. What methods will you use? How will you make sure you're interpreting things correctly? What passages will you tackle?

STEP TWO: Act!

We're assuming that you actually did attempt to study the Bible in a more complete way. If so, did it go as you had planned? Was it easier or harder than you expected? What difference did it make in your Bible study?

STEP THREE: Review!

Do you think you interpreted Scripture in the way it was meant to be interpreted? Next time you study a passage, what will you do differently? Do you feel any different about Bible study now? If so, how?

LITTLE BIBLE BACKGROUND

Link 1

What things have you heard or thought about the Bible that turned out not to be true? How did it make you feel to know that you were wrong about God's Word? Do you believe there are still some things about the Bible you may be misunderstanding without even realizing it? Explain that the purpose of this session is to clear up some biblical misunderstandings.

Link 2

Explain: **I'm going to name some common mistakes people make in trying to understand God's Word. As I read each one, tell me how that mistake could affect the way a person understands the Bible.** Feel free to add your own suggestions to this list:
• Assuming that you know what a passage is saying after reading it once.
• Assuming that the Bible has nothing specific to say about modern life.
• Assuming that the Bible is a list of dos and don'ts.

ADVANCED LEARNERS

Link 2

Have one of your students read Matthew 13:1-9. Then put this question to your group members: **Why was it hard for Pharisees to understand what Jesus was talking about?** If your students are stumped for an answer, refer them to Matthew 13:10-35.

Link 3

If your advanced group members finish the "practice passage" in time, give them another one to try: Matthew 5:27-30. Use the following questions to guide your discussion of the passage:
• What might happen if you misunderstood this passage?
• What kind of guidance would you ask the Holy Spirit for?
• What more can we find out about who Jesus was talking to, what the circumstances were, or anything else that might help us understand the passage better?
• Why do you suppose Jesus called for such extreme measures?
• Can you think of any other verses that talk about resisting temptation? If so, what do they say?
• Who would you go to with your questions about this passage? What specifically would you ask?
• What changes would you make in your life as a result of what you learned about this passage?

MOSTLY GUYS

Link 1

Put these questions to your guys: **Have you ever embarrassed yourself by misreading the signals a girl was sending you? If so, what happened? How did you feel?** Share some embarrassing encounters of your own, if you have any. Then ask: **Besides our relationship with the opposite sex, what are some other areas of life in which getting the right message is important?**

Link 3

If you've got a group made up entirely of guys, you might want to substitute the "practice passage" in Step 3 with 1 Corinthians 7:1. Use the following questions to guide your discussion of the passage:

• What might happen if you misunderstood this verse?

• What kind of guidance would you ask the Holy Spirit for?

• What more can we find out about who Paul was talking to, what the circumstances were, or anything else that might help us understand the verse better?

• Why do you think Paul felt that way?

• Can you think of any other verses that talk about marriage? If so, what do they say?

• Who would you go to with your questions about this verse? What specifically would you ask?

• What changes would you make in your way of thinking as a result of what you learned about this verse?

MOSTLY GIRLS

Link 1

Put these questions to your girls: **Do you ever worry about sending the wrong signals to a guy? What are some signals that a guy might take the wrong way? How do you avoid sending the wrong signals?** Ask volunteers to share their experiences with inadvertently sending the wrong message to a guy. Then ask: **Besides our relationship with the opposite sex, what are some other areas of life in which getting the right message is important?**

Link 3

If you've got a group made up entirely of girls, you might want to substitute the "practice passage" in Step 3 with 1 Corinthians 7:29. Use the following questions to guide your discussion of the passage:

• What might happen if you misunderstood this passage?

• What kind of guidance would you ask the Holy Spirit for?

• What more can we find out about who Paul was talking to, what the circumstances were, or anything else that might help us understand the passage better?

• Why do you think Paul put such restrictions on the Corinthian women?

• Can you think of any other verses that talk about women and marriage? If so, what do they say?

• Who would you go to with your questions about this passage? What specifically would you ask?

• What changes would you make in your way of thinking as a result of what you learned about this passage?

MEDIA

Link 1

Needed: Recording of some older songs and a tape or CD player

Bring in a tape of some well-known songs with hard-to-understand lyrics. (Oldies like "Louie, Louie" by The Kingsmen and "Jumpin' Jack Flash" by The Rolling Stones are good examples.) Play the songs for your students and let them try to decipher the lyrics. Afterward, ask: **Do you ever have trouble understanding other things in life—some Bible verses, for example?**

Link 2

Needed: Video of *The Ten Commandments, The Greatest Story Ever Told,* video player and TV

Bring in a video of *The Ten Commandments, The Greatest Story Ever Told,* or some other biblical epic. Fast-forward to the middle of the movie and play five seconds of a scene. Ask your group members to identify who the characters on screen are and what they're doing. Unless you land on a pretty obvious clip, your students will likely have trouble figuring out what's going on in the film.

Afterward, ask: **Why was it so hard to figure out what was going on?** (We saw only a small portion of the movie. We didn't know what had happened before the scene. We had no context for the scene.)

EXTRA ADRENALINE

Link 1

Needed: Old magazines and a list of homophones

Here's a game based on the same principles of misunderstanding as the questions in Step 1. All you'll need is a stack of old magazines and a list of homophones, words that sound alike but have different meanings (blue-blew, red-read, sew-sow). Give each a player a few magazines. Explain that when you call out a word or phrase, the contestants will have to find something that matches it in their magazines, tear it out, and bring it to you. Explain: **For example, if I were to say, "Current," you would have to find something that might be considered current in your magazine and bring it to me.**

What your group members won't know until the game begins, though, is that you'll be using homophones from your list. So, rather than looking for something current, you'll be looking for something currant, which is fruit used for jelly. The first person to bring you a picture of something like a jelly jar, then, would win. After you've played a few rounds and students have figured out what you're looking for, ask: **In what other areas of life is correct understanding extremely important?**

Link 3

Use the five steps as five stations for "Speed Studying" the quickest way to understand the Bible. Set up five different destinations for the group, as you run from one step to the other after the students have discussed each step. Make sure you don't rush the discussion of the verse, just the ways you transition from one step to another.

JUNIOR HIGH

Link 1

Begin the session with a game of "Telephone." Line your group members up in a single file line. Whisper a long message (perhaps an obscure Bible verse or a portion of the Gettysburg Address) to the first person in line. Speak as quickly as you can and do not repeat the message. The person you whisper to will then pass along what he heard to the next person in line. The message will continue being passed from person to person until it reaches the end of the line. Compare the final version of the message with the original. Chances are, it will be quite different. Afterward, ask: **What caused the misunderstanding in this game? What causes misunderstandings in our everyday lives?**

Link 3

Explain: **One of the best ways to figure out what's going on in a Bible passage is to imagine ourselves in the Bible setting and to use our five senses to describe what's happening.** Ask your students to turn to Matthew 8:23-27. After they've read the passage, ask these questions:

• **Putting yourself on the boat, what things do you see?** (Dark clouds, lightning, dangerous waves)

- **What do you hear?** (Thunder, crashing waves, screaming men)
- **What do you taste?** (Saltwater, rain)
- **What do you feel?** (Seasickness, rocking boat, chilliness)
- **What do you smell?** (Fish, body odor)

Point out that not all passages lend themselves to this kind of study, but that we should always try to put ourselves as close as we can to the action in Scripture.

Planning Checklist

LINK 1: There Must Be Some Misunderstanding
- ❑ Little Bible Background
- ❑ Mostly Guys
- ❑ Mostly Girls
- ❑ Media
- ❑ Extra Adrenaline
- ❑ Junior High

LINK 2: Jesus Clears It Up
- ❑ Little Bible Background
- ❑ Advanced Learners
- ❑ Media

LINK 3: For Demonstration Purposes Only
- ❑ Advanced Learners
- ❑ Mostly Guys
- ❑ Mostly Girls
- ❑ Extra Adrenaline
- ❑ Junior High

PASS IT ON

KEY QUESTIONS

- What effect can God's Word have in a person's life?
- What instructions did Jesus give His followers regarding spreading His Word?
- What are the most effective ways to witness to God's Word?

BIBLE BASE

Matthew 5:14-16
Matthew 28:16-20
John 1:14

SUPPLIES

- Paper
- Bibles
- Attention-getter of your choice (Opener)
- Copies of Resources 4A, 4B, Journal
- Pencils

Opener (Optional)

Did You See That?

This opener will require a little work on your part, but if you do it right, you'll set the tone for an extremely effective session. Have something interesting or unusual in the parking lot when your group members arrive. It could be anything from a brand new Ferrari to a man in bunny costume dancing the Watusi to imaginary music, as long as it gets your group members' attention.

LEARNER LINK

If you don't have the chance to find an attention getter like those described in the opener, kick off by asking the students to describe a time when they met someone famous. Who was it and what was it like? Use the follow up discussion questions in the opener to make the connection to an exciting event, and then wanting to share it with others.

MAKING IT REAL

One of the benefits of leading a small discipleship group is the chance to reach out to some of the parents and families of the students. Make a point, any chance you get, to talk with them and to let them know what you have been doing in your group. Parents appreciate that and it can help them encourage their teens at home. Not all of the parents may be Christians so be aware that they are looking for the characteristics of Jesus in your life.

Before you start the meeting, pay attention to your group members' conversations. Make a mental note of their excitement to share what they witnessed. Also make a note of the reaction of those who didn't witness the spectacle. How do they respond? Are they skeptical? Are they drawn in by the description?

Discuss your observations briefly at the beginning of the meeting, using the following questions:
- For those of you who witnessed the "spectacle" earlier, why were you so anxious to share what you saw?
- Were you worried about people not believing you? Why or why not?
- For those of you who didn't witness it, what did you think of the reports you heard?
- What's the best way to get someone's attention with news like this?

Introduce the session this way: **Today we'll be talking about sharing God's Word with people who haven't heard much about it before. While that may not seem as exciting as the news you just shared, it is much more important.**

Link 1

Newsworthy

If you handed out Resource 3C at the end of Session 3, take a few minutes at the beginning of this meeting to find out how your students' attempts at interpreting Scripture went. Ask volunteers to share their experiences, both positive and negative, with the rest of the group. Encourage other group members to comment on the volunteers' experiences. Remember, your goal is to develop an atmosphere in which everyone feels comfortable enough to be completely open and honest.

Hand out copies of "Something to Talk About" (Resource 4A). Give group members a few minutes to fill out the sheet. When they're finished, ask volunteers to talk about how they ranked each item and why. Focus especially on the last item, "The Bible has made a big difference in my life."

Ask: **Can you think of a situation in which you'd be really excited to tell someone about how God's Word has helped you?** Get a few responses to find out how strongly your group members feel about sharing (or not sharing) God's Word with other people.

Do you always have to share a Scripture or explain the plan of salvation to share your faith? (No.)

God draws people to Himself in many different ways. In fact, each one of you in this room has a unique story about when and how you became a Christian. Ask for volunteers to share the story of how they came to know Christ. If you have time, consider sharing your story too.

Over the past three weeks we've been studying about how to be disciples of Jesus. Another part of being a disciple is sharing God's love and His Word. There is no one "right way" to share your faith. Your boldness coupled with the Holy Spirit's work in you and in other people is an unbeatable combination.

Link 2

Famous Last Words

Kick off the Bible study portion of your meeting with this question: **Who can tell me what Jesus' last words on earth were?** If no one is able to come up with the answer, ask one of your group members to read aloud Matthew 28:16-20.

Point out: **Since these are Jesus' last words, they're probably pretty important. What is He saying to His followers in these verses?** (He's instructing us to take the message that we received from Him to people all over the world. He's instructing us to make disciples of others in the same way that we were made disciples. He's asking us to spread the news of what He did and what He continues to do for us every day.)

What do Jesus' final instructions have to do with God's Word? (Everything we need to tell others about Jesus and the Christian life is found in Scripture. Talking to other people about God's Word is one of the best ways to fulfill Jesus' instructions.)

Sharing God's Word with "all nations" seems like a pretty big job. How can we even hope to accomplish Jesus' mission for us? (Some missionaries travel throughout the world, but if disciples everywhere concentrated on their own small part of the world, it's likely that the whole world would eventually hear of God's Word.)

If you were to follow Jesus' command and start telling other people about God's Word, where would you begin? If no one mentions it, suggest that starting with the people closest to us is probably the best strategy. There's less chance of outright rejection if we concentrate on family members, friends, and neighbors to begin with. Then, after we've gained confidence and experience, we can move on to people we don't know as well.

Now move into a fuller discussion of what it means to witness to God's Word. Make the point that it is more than just what we *say*. In fact, Jesus shows us that it also involves two more aspects of our lives.

Have a volunteer read aloud Matthew 5:14-16. Ask:
• **How is a shining light like the good deeds of Christians?** (People see the light, just as they see our actions. Our actions tell about our priorities, our loves, our desires, our relationships. Good and loving actions spread the message of God's goodness and love in our lives.)
• **How can we make our lights shine brighter? dimmer?** (We can openly act for the good, even when those actions go against the crowd. Or we can act like the things of God do not matter to us.)
• **What is Jesus telling us about an important way of witnessing?** (He's telling us that it's more than what we say; it also involves how we live our lives.)

Have a volunteer read aloud John 1:14. Ask:
• **Who is Jesus, in essence?** (He is the eternal Word; God in the flesh.)
• **Because of who He is, what do people see?** (They see His greatness and glory; they see His character of grace and truth.)
• **How is this verse a statement about witnessing, even though no one is talking?** (It tells us that *who* we are "speaks" about *whose* we are!)
• **How is what you are, day in and day out, a "speech" about the Word?**

Link 3

Test Run

Explain: **We've talked about the whats and whys of sharing God's Word with others. Now let's talk about the hows of the "saying" part of witnessing. We're going to practice sharing God's Word with two people who really need to hear it. And to make things a little easier for you, we've even given you the verses you need.**

Hand out copies of "Worth Sharing" (Resource 4B). Let group members work in pairs to complete the sheet. After a few minutes, ask volunteers to share what they came up with. Use the following information and questions to guide your discussion:

Rachel
The one thing Rachel needs in her life is stability, someone or something she can depend on. Her parents' divorce has caused her to question whether anything is permanent. Hebrews 13:8 tells us of a Person who is not susceptible to whims and changing feelings. Jesus, and the love He has for His people, will never change. Likewise, the eternal home He is preparing for His followers cannot be spoiled by anything.

How could you introduce these passages to Rachel without seeming like a religious nut or scaring her away? (The key is to be sensitive to her needs. Do not underestimate her pain or overestimate the immediate effect the Bible will have on her life. Be realistic. You might say something like this: "I know you're probably going to be up most of the night thinking about things. If you are, I've got something I want you to read. It's really short, but it's helped me through some tough times, and I think it might help you.") **What's the worst thing that could happen if you tried to share God's Word with Rachel? What would be the best thing that could happen if you talked to Rachel about God's Word?**

Andy
More than anything else, Andy is concerned about the future—his future and his family's future. Matthew 6:25-34 and 1 Corinthians 2:9-10 describe God's love and concern for His creation. Nothing—not even financial ruin—can interfere with the future plans He has for our lives.

How could you introduce these passages to Andy without making him uncomfortable? (Perhaps one of the best things you could do for Andy would be to share some of your own fears and concerns about the future. Chances are, you won't have a story like his, but that shouldn't stop you from telling him about your own struggles. You'll also want to talk about the comfort and direction you've received from God and His Word concerning your future.) **What's the worst thing that could happen if you tried to share God's Word with Andy? What would be the best thing that could happen if you talked to Andy about God's Word?**

Maybe you won't be talking to people with problems as serious as Rachel's and Andy's. What are some other situations people you know may be facing? Your group members may name anything from broken hearts to poor grades to self-image problems.

What can we do to share God's Word in those situations? (Look for needs in other people's lives, find passages that fit those needs, be good listeners, have the guts to share, prepare ourselves for both positive and negative reactions.)

LEARNER LINK

It might be helpful for students to roleplay a sharing session. When you are actually talking to someone, it is significantly different from just thinking about what you are going to say. Have one volunteer pretend to be Rachel and have another volunteer be the friend who wants to help. If you have time roleplay both situations two times. Have the volunteers playing Rachel and Andy respond in a positive way and a negative way. If you don't have time for all of these just pick one or make a new one up. Remind students that having the "right" words to say to a person is not something to get nervous about. God will get His point across in the best way for each individual. Our job is to pray for the person, have a right heart before God, and be bold.

MAKING IT REAL

Don't give your students the impression that it's easy to follow Jesus' example! If you don't acknowledge the challenges, some of your group members may leave with unrealistic expectations. Prepare your students for the unfortunate possibilities by talking honestly about how people may respond to them and risks involved in being a disciple of Jesus Christ. Rather than discouraging your group members, you may find that your straightforward approach actually motivates many of them.

What would it take for you to begin sharing God's Word with other people this week? Encourage most, if not all, of your group members to respond. Specifically, ask them to close their eyes—just for a minute—and envision one person they know who could benefit from their witness. Have them begin imagining how the conversation might go.

As you wrap up your discussion, hand out copies of "Heart Check: A Practical Approach to Telling Others about God's Word" (Resource 4C). Have students spend some time in class answering the questions under the "Plan!" section of "Do It Up"—the last part of the worksheet.

Then have your students get together with their accountability partners and share their plans. They should commit to praying for each other this week concerning the plans they just made. Also have students pray together now or bring them back to a large group and pray for the commitments they just made. Encourage your students to set aside a few minutes each day to work on the sheet and follow through on their "action plans."

Something to Talk About

Rate the following messages on a scale of 1 to 5, according to how urgent you think they are or how quickly you would want to tell others about them.

5 = Alert the media and everyone I've ever met!
4 = I can't wait to tell my friends about it.
3 = It could wait until tomorrow.
2 = I might mention it someday.
1 = I'll keep it to myself.

© PhotoDisc, Inc.

_____ MY GRANDPARENTS WON THE LOTTERY.

_____ I FOUND $20 IN THE POCKET OF MY JACKET.

_____ I GOT AN "A" ON MY HISTORY FINAL.

_____ THE PERSON I'VE BEEN DYING TO DATE SAT NEXT TO ME AT LUNCH.

_____ I HAD TO GO TO THE EMERGENCY ROOM.

_____ I SAW TOM CRUISE AT THE MALL.

_____ I GOT AN OBSCENE PHONE CALL.

_____ MY PARENTS TOLD ME THEY'RE BUYING ME A CAR FOR MY BIRTHDAY.

_____ I WAS INTERVIEWED BY A TV NEWS REPORTER.

_____ THE BIBLE HAS MADE A BIG DIFFERENCE IN MY LIFE.

Worth Sharing

Below you'll find descriptions of two people facing serious problems in their lives. You'll also find Bible passages that deal with those problems. You've got two people in need of God's Word. Unfortunately, neither of them fully understands that need. Your job is to help them recognize their need and then show them how Scripture can help them, regardless of their circumstances.

Read each of the following personal descriptions, look up the passages listed below it, and then write down how you would explain that passage, using words anyone can understand, in light of the person's situation or circumstances.

RACHEL

Divorce. That was the only word that really stuck with Rachel. Her mom kept going on and on about how "this was the best thing for everyone involved" and about how "this doesn't mean your father and I don't love you" and about how "sometimes people just grow apart." Blah, blah, blah. That's what the rest of it sounded like to Rachel.

Not much else registered with Rachel right away. Not the pain, not the anger, not the feelings of betrayal or worthlessness—though those would all come later. The only thing Rachel knew at that moment was that she could never be completely secure about anything in her life again. If her parents' marriage couldn't last forever, nothing could.

That thought made Rachel more scared than she had ever been in her life.

Knowing what you know about Rachel, how would you explain Hebrews 13:8 and 1 Peter 1:3-4 to her?

ANDY

Andy didn't know exactly what bankruptcy was when his father first mentioned it. He knew it was bad, of course. But he didn't know how bad.

Once upon a time, Andy's father had been a successful executive at a large publishing company. But then he decided to start his own company and become a publisher himself. There's no need to mention all of the problems his new company faced. Let's just say anything that could go wrong did. For two years his father struggled, sacrificed, and poured his own money into the company. But it was no use. The company dissolved, along with the family's finances and most of their possessions.

Now, neither Andy nor his family has any idea of what lies ahead. His father may find another job, but what will the family do in the meantime? They may find an apartment to live in for a while, but what about the future? Perhaps most importantly, what will Andy do after he graduates next year? His college fund was wiped out.

Knowing what you know about Andy, how would you explain Matthew 6:25-34 and 1 Corinthians 2:9-10 to him?

HEART CHECK:
A Practical Approach to Telling Others about God's Word

You may think you've picked up some valuable tips for sharing God's Word with other people, but unless you actually put them to use in your life these tips are worthless. Remember, God wants not only "listeners" of His Word, but "doers" (James 1:22). This sheet is for doers.

LOOK IT UP

Below you'll find seven Scripture references, one for every day of the week. Each passage listed below has something interesting to say about sharing God's Word with others. Spend a few minutes each day looking up the passage and writing down a few (relevant) thoughts that pop into your head.

DAY ONE: Matthew 5:14-16 (What does it mean to let our light shine before other people?)

_____
_____
_____
_____

DAY TWO: Mark 8:38 (What do you think it means to be ashamed of the Lord?)

_____
_____
_____
_____

DAY THREE: Luke 2:8-20 (How do you think the shepherds explained what they had seen?)

_____
_____
_____
_____

DAY FOUR: 2 Corinthians 4:3-6 (How does Satan blind people to the truth of the gospel?)

_____
_____
_____
_____

☺ TALK IT UP

Jesus tells us that "all things are possible with God" (Mark 10:27). That includes telling people about His Word. So when we're faced with a really difficult situation, like sharing a passage with someone who's hurting, a wise first step is to consult the One who makes all things possible. Take some time to write down a few prayer requests, specific ways in which you need the Lord to help you. (For example, you might ask Him to give you strength and courage when you attempt to talk about the Bible with people who may not be interested in hearing about it.) Don't be afraid to get personal here. No one else needs to see your prayer request list.

_____
_____
_____
_____
_____
_____
_____
_____
_____
_____
_____
_____
_____
_____
_____

DAY FIVE: Ephesians 4:14-16 (What does it mean to speak the truth in love?)

_____

_____

_____

_____

DAY SIX: Matthew 10:32-33 (What are some ways in which we can acknowledge the Lord before other people?)

_____

_____

_____

_____

DAY SEVEN: 1 Peter 2:12 (What kinds of things might catch the attention of "pagans" and cause them to consider the Lord?)

_____

_____

_____

_____

DO IT UP

If you're serious about following the biblical examples of telling others about God's Word, you'll need an action plan. Here is one to follow.

STEP ONE: **Plan!**

What are you going to do this week to share God's Word with someone who needs to hear about it? Put some thought into your response. Be specific. How exactly will you bring up the topic? When will you do it? How will you deal with the person's reaction?

STEP TWO: **Act!**

Put your plan into action and then answer these questions. Did it go as you planned? What did you end up doing? How did you feel right before you started the conversation? Was it easier or harder than you expected?

STEP THREE: **Review!**

Do you think you handled the situation in a God-honoring way? If you had a chance to do it over again, what would you do differently?

LITTLE BIBLE BACKGROUND

Link 2

Draw an abstract figure on the board. The figure should be made up entirely of common shapes like squares, circles, triangles, ovals, and rectangles. Keep the drawing covered for the first part of your meeting. When you're ready to use it, ask one of your group members, preferably someone with some artistic ability, to sit facing away from the board. Give this person a pencil and piece of paper. Remove the cover from your drawing. Ask another group member to describe the figure on the board while the first person attempts to draw it. The artist will take his cues entirely from his partner's description. When the two are finished with their collaboration, compare the drawing with the original to see how well the partners did re-creating it.

Afterward, ask: **Do you ever feel this way when you're trying to explain the Bible to someone else? How hard is it to describe God's Word to people who have no idea what it is? What kind of responsibility do you feel, knowing that other people's view of the Bible depends on what you say?**

Link 3

As you focus your group members' attention on practical ways to share the Bible with other people, ask them this question: **What do you wish someone had told you about the Bible?** Using their own experience as a jumping off point, ask your group members to come up with a strategy for telling people exactly what they need to hear about God's Word.

ADVANCED LEARNERS

Link 2

Needed: Tracts from several different denominations and churches

Bring in a collection of tracts from several different denominations and churches. If possible, make sure that the entire spectrum of Christianity is represented in your material. Try to collect pieces from as many churches as possible. Distribute the tracts among your group members, giving them several minutes to read as many different ones as they can. Afterward, ask volunteers to share their opinions of the different pieces, which ones worked for them and which ones didn't.

Discuss the tracts, using these questions: **What is the purpose of a tract? Do you think tracts are a good way to communicate what the Bible says? Why or why not? If you were going to make a tract, what would it look like? What kind of message would it include?**

Link 3

Put these questions to your group members who have grown up in the church: **How many of you know what a cliché is?** (It's a word or phrase that's been used so often that it's become a stereotype and lost much of its meaning.)

Can you think of any Christian clichés, words or phrases used all the time by believers that have little meaning outside of Christian circles? If your group members need help, suggest that even such "basic" words as saved, witnessing, and fellowship have little meaning to people outside the church.

How might clichés interfere in our efforts to talk to others about the Bible? (If we don't use language all people can understand, we'll probably be "tuned out.")

What are some strategies we can use to avoid speaking in clichés when we talk to others about the Bible? Encourage your group members to be creative with their answers.

MOSTLY GUYS

Link 2

Put this question to your guys: **What would you say is the most popular topic of conversation among most of the guys you know?** It's likely that many of your group members will name "sports" as the primary topic of conversation. Don't worry if they come up with another answer. The next questions still apply just substitute the topic your group picked.

Continue the conversation with these questions: **What is it about sports that's so interesting to guys in particular?** (Many guys thrive on the action and competition that sports provide—to the point that they even enjoy talking about it.)

How could we use some of these same principles to talk about the Bible with our friends? There are all kinds of ideas you can explore here: the action-oriented nature of Jesus' life, the "race" that is set before Christians, Satan's competitive nature against God, etc. Emphasize to your group members the importance of speaking to people on terms they can relate to.

Link 3

Read a list of activities that your guys normally participate in, and ask them to tell you which ones present the best opportunities for talking about the Bible and why. Here is a list of some activities you might name: a pick-up basketball game, cruising around in a car, band practice, a round of golf, etc. After you've determined which activities lend themselves to Bible discussions, talk about some strategies for beginning those discussions.

MOSTLY GIRLS

Link 2

Needed: Index cards with a Bible verse written in several different languages

Before the session, you'll need to write out a well-known Bible passage in several different languages, with each version on its own index card. You'll probably be able to find foreign-language Bibles in your local library or Christian bookstore. Hand out the cards at your meeting and ask your group members to do their best at reading the foreign translations. When everyone is finished reading, have your girls try to guess what the passage is. To begin your discussion of the activity, ask: **Besides using the right language, what are some other ways we can adjust our conversations about the Bible to make sure that people understand what we're saying?**

Link 3

Explain: **I'm going to read a list of strategies for beginning conversations about God's Word. Tell me which ones you think would work for you and why.** Encourage your girls to be specific in their explanations. After you've gone through the following list, ask group members to suggest some additional strategies.

- Playing Christian music in your car.
- Carrying a Bible around with you at school.
- Wearing a Christian T-shirt.
- Living such a clean life that others have to ask you about it.
- Praying silently before lunch.

MEDIA

Link 2

Needed: Videotape of clips from Christian shows, video player and TV

Before the meeting, you'll need to record snippets from several different Christian TV programs. These snippets, which should be no longer than thirty seconds apiece, should run the gamut from serious Bible studies to laughable televangelists. Show the clips to your group members. Ask them to identify which ones they think would be most effective in reaching their non-Christian friends and why. Afterward, ask: **Which strategies do *you* find most effective for starting conversations about the Bible?** Encourage several group members to share their opinions and experiences.

Link 3

Needed: Videotape of commercials, video player and TV

While you're taping clips from Christian television shows (see Step 2 above), take some time to record some commercials as well. If possible, try to get a sampling of several different kinds of commercials—infomercials, humorous spots, public service announcements, etc. Show the clips to your group members. Ask your students, then, to create their own commercial—using one of the formats they just saw—to explain what the Bible has to offer. Let your group members work in pairs on their commercials. When they're finished, ask each pair to explain or perform its commercial.

EXTRA ADRENALINE

Link 1

Needed: Blindfold for each group member

Kick things off with a game called "Bible Find." All you'll need for the game is a Bible and a blindfold for each group member. After your students have their blindfolds in place, hide the Bible somewhere in the room. Let your students wander around the room blindly, using their hands to try to find the Bible. If you hide the Bible well enough—and if no one peeks—your students shouldn't be able to find it.

After a few minutes, call time and pair up your group members for the second round. In this round, one blindfolded member of each pair will try to find the hidden Bible again. This time, however, she will be guided by her non-blindfolded partner, who knows where the Bible is and will attempt to guide her there, using specific instructions ("Take two baby steps to the left, then three giant steps forward"). It's likely that your players will find this round much easier than the first one.

Afterward, ask: **What can this game teach us about sharing God's Word with other people?** (Many people are stumbling around in the dark, not knowing where to turn to for guidance and comfort in their lives. They need someone who can direct them to the truth of God's Word.)

Link 3

Needed: Adult volunteer

Announce: **I have a treat for you today. Our special guest is an alien from another solar system.** Bring in an adult volunteer, preferably someone who is quick thinking and comfortable interacting with students. **As a group, we're going to try to explain the main message of God's Word to him. The problem is, he knows absolutely nothing about it—and I do mean *nothing*.**

This activity should prove to be challenging, fun, and frustrating to your group members. For example, if they start their explanation with God's creation of the universe, your "alien" will ask (in his best alien voice), "What is God?" Your group members will soon find that even their most basic explanations assume some kind of knowledge on the part of the listener. When that knowledge isn't there, they may be lost in trying to find an alternative explanation.

Afterward, ask: **What can we learn from this encounter about trying to talk to people about God's Word?** (Sometimes it's best to assume that the person knows nothing about it. Therefore, we should use words that everybody can understand.)

JUNIOR HIGH

Link 1

Choose one of your group members to serve as the "communicator." You will whisper a message in the person's ear—something like, "The brownies are poisoned." That person will then be responsible for spreading the message to the rest of the group without speaking and *without* using his arms, hands, or fingers. This should make it difficult, but not impossible, for the person to communicate. After the game, ask: **How did it feel to you not to be able to communicate in a way that people understand? How difficult is it to talk about God's Word with people who don't understand what we're saying?**

Link 3

End your meeting with an interactive roleplay. Let your junior highers practice their discussion techniques in real-life settings. Ask for two volunteers for the roleplay. One person will play a Christian trying to start a conversation about the Bible. The other person will play his non-Christian friend. See how well your "Christian" role-players do at starting conversations. After each roleplay, let the rest of the group offer comments and suggestions.

Planning Checklist

OPENER: Did You See That?
❏ Junior High

LINK 1: Newsworthy
❏ Extra Adrenaline

LINK 2: Famous Last Words
❏ Little Bible Background
❏ Advanced Learners
❏ Mostly Guys
❏ Mostly Girls
❏ Media

LINK 3: Test Run
❏ Little Bible Background
❏ Advanced Learners
❏ Mostly Guys
❏ Mostly Girls
❏ Media
❏ Extra Adrenaline
❏ Junior High

REALITY CHECK: GOD'S WORD MAKES A DIFFERENCE

About This Session

This bonus session is designed to help your group members understand discipleship in a deeper, more hands-on way. The four sessions of this book cover what it means to love God's Word as Jesus did and become His disciple. True discipleship involves the heart, the head, and the hands. During this session you'll give your students a chance to take the things that they are learning and experiencing and put them into practice in the real world. This experiential learning time is a good way to wrap up your four weeks of study, but it can also be done at any point throughout the study.

Check it Out

As a group, have your students brainstorm together ways that God's Word is taught to others. One of the easiest settings to picture will probably be a type of Sunday school for children youth, or adults. Ask your students to remember back to the times they went to Sunday school. Ask what they remember about the teacher, the room, the activities, etc.

A great suggestion is to have students help out with a Sunday school class for younger children. This may be a great way for your students to get involved in helping others understand and apply God's Word. They could offer their services in preparing supplies in advance, and then be there in the classroom to help the children put projects together. Encourage your teens to approach this with a servant's attitude, being ready to help the teacher in any way possible.

Take it Deeper

If you feel your students are ready for a deeper commitment, have them: actually prepare and teach the children's Sunday school class for a particular week, giving the teachers a complete break. Be sure to emphasize that this is an excellent way to learn from, interpret, memorize, and proclaim God's Word—putting into action all the things they've been studying!

After the lesson is over you might take this even deeper by having your students interview a veteran Sunday school teacher. Have your group come up with some open-ended questions and pick someone who has been a teacher, discipler, or leader for at least five years. The object here would be to give students a chance to hear stories of how God has worked in this teacher's life. Students should ask things concerning how God has worked in student's lives as well as the teacher's life. The more stories the better—this should give your students a glimpse of God's wondrous variety and creativity.

Think it Through

Ideally you will spend most of your debriefing time listening to your group members' experiences in the "real world." Encourage your students to share their feelings about helping and sharing with people they don't know. If you need some discussion guides, use any or all of the following questions.

• Based on your experience, how good would you say you are at recognizing and meeting other people's needs?

• Was your experience what you expected it to be? If so what did you expect? If not, how was it different? Were you pleasantly surprised or a little disappointed? Explain.

• How much do you think the teacher or students appreciated your help? Why?

• Why is it important for us to help other people understand God's Word?

• What are some other ways you can help people understand God's Word?

• What's the most important thing you learned from your experience of helping teachers and working with children in Sunday school?

Close the meeting (and this study) with a word of prayer. Thank God for your group members and their willingness to commit themselves to discipleship in a world in which disciples are all-too-rare. Ask God to help your students continue to make His Word accessible and meaningful to others.

Name	Address	Phone	Parent Names	e-mail	B-day	Notes
1.						
2.						
3.						
4.						
5.						
6.						
7.						
8.						
9.						
10.						
11.						
12.						
13.						
14.						
15.						

Lift IT UP

Ephesians 3:16 "I pray that out of his glorious riches he may strengthen you with power through his Spirit in your inner being, so that Christ may dwell in your hearts through faith. And I pray that you, being rooted and established in love, may have power, together with all the saints to grasp how wide and long and high and deep is the love of Christ, and to know this love that surpasses knowledge—that you may be filled to the measure of all the fullness of God."